AUG 02 1992

W9-AUD-622

979.49   Highland, Monica.

Greetings from
Southern
California.

$24.95

DATE			

WITHDRAWN

L   113

BAKER & TAYLOR BOOKS

Greetings from Seal Beach, Cal.

Happy Days by the Glad Sea Waves!   3356

c. 1910

Greetings from Southern California

by Monica Highland

GRAPHIC ARTS CENTER PUBLISHING COMPANY, PORTLAND, OREGON

VALENCIA LIBRARY
23743 W. Valencia Blvd.
Valencia, Calif. 91355-2191
(805) 259-8942

Lakeside — San Diego Co., Cal.

c. 1910

International Standard Book Number 0-932575-71-4
Library of Congress Catalog Number 88-80472
Copyright ©MCMLXXXVIII by Graphic Arts Center Publishing Company
P.O. Box 10306, Portland, Oregon 97210 • 503/226-2402
Editor-in-Chief • Douglas A. Pfeiffer
Illustrations Assistant • Alison Morba
Designer • Robert Reynolds
Typographer • Harrison Typesetting, Inc.
Color Separations • Graphic Arts Center, Inc.
Printer • Dynagraphics, Inc.
Binder • Lincoln & Allen

Printed in the United States of America

To the memory of George Newton Bowlin Laws, who collected many of them; to Mary Frances Espey McAllister, who, happily, still sends them; and to Stella Louise Copeland See, who, as a girl, frisked through these halcyon landscapes.

A special debt of gratitude is owed to the deltiologists whose extraordinary postcard collections and enduring affection for Southern California have made this book possible: JoAnn Hilston, Gisela Granstrom, Lee Brown, Carolyn See, Paul Oncidi, Marian and Peter Maronn.

The postcard on page 107 is © The Walt Disney Company and is reprinted in this book with their permission.

I'LL EAT ORANGES FOR YOU
YOU THROW SNOW BALLS FOR ME

c. 1910

CONTENTS

Circa dates refer to a ten-year time period largely determined by the printing styles of a particular era, the subject matter depicted, and other information providing clues to a card's actual date of publication.

Penny Dreams

12691 ALMOND TREES IN BLOSSOM, RIVERSIDE, CALIF.   COPR. DETROIT PHOTOGRAPHIC CO.

c. 1920

Southern California postcards reflect a particular vision of the world—a romantic, idealized, often whimsical, dream. Some people may amuse themselves by "dating" these cards from the costumes or the cars or even the size of the palm trees outside the Santa Barbara Mission. Others may marvel at the extraordinary natural wonders these cards record. But the discerning observer will see these cards as a genuine art form. Like popular songs that remain in your memory, these cards encapsulate a particular moment; each is a jeweled bead in the necklace of time.

Of course, the entrepreneur saw it differently. In 1969, N. R. "Nat" Sherman, owner of the Western Publishing and Novelty Company, briskly informed a reporter that, before 1940, "the reproduction really wasn't worth talking about, it wasn't good. From 1940 to 1950, the linen finish gave you your best card. After that came Kodachrome and everything changed." He reminisced that, "in the old days, a photographer would wait for hours for the right light, the right clouds, then sell a card for between 15 and 25 dollars and never see a royalty on his work." Sherman recalled that during World War II, paper rationing did not apply to the postcard industry—so essential were these souvenirs in keeping up the morale of the troops scattered around the world. He noted that "a good drugstore in a good location might sell from 3,000 to 5,000 postcards a year. . . . An image of Olvera Street alone sold 3,000 a year, but Dodger Stadium was falling off." Sherman, however, was only a typical hard-headed businessman who daily faced the vagaries of the marketplace, and postcards were a commodity.

Collectors—among them, George Laws—loved them with all their hearts. In that same year, 1969, Laws explained postcards in quite a different way. "They are beautiful," he said, stroking his tinted beard. "Beautiful in a way which nothing else quite matches. It's as if you saw an idiot actor who never made more than $70 a week playing his heart out at the. . . Crescent Theater in a town you never heard of. Do you understand me? The artists who created these cards, by and large, had no formal education. They saw what they thought of as beautiful and set about to record it. They knew they'd never get rich but they also knew their work would end up all over the nation. Those early postcards were like valentines, sent from their own hearts."

Where Sherman dismissed the early cards, Laws recalled that the earliest cards were "lithographed on stone. . . . The best work was done by the Detroit and Leighton Companies. They are as pretty as any gorgeous color engraving from Europe. . . ."

Like many other collectors, George Laws had an eye for the unusual—even the bizarre. "Once," he said, "I had a postcard of the San Diego Quarantine Station. There wasn't one house or one battleship. I made it out to be 1906 or before. I used to have San Pedro Harbor, but the only steam vessel was a tug. The harbor was jammed with ships, but they're sailing ships, tall ships. And what the artists did for California! There was *never* such a blue sky as the ones they tinted in! Take a look at those oranges, those bright blue hydrangeas, those blushing nubile beauties in the Rose Parade! How about all those dead *sharks* lined up on the beach at Catalina? It was unbelievable. I mean, I wonder what they thought in Red Oak, Iowa, when they got those cards. . . . Let's just say," Laws charitably summed up, "some of those photographers and artists had more enthusiasm than sense."

MAIN STREET, LOOKING SOUTH, OCEANSIDE, CALIFORNIA—203

c. 1940

By The Glad Sea Waves

Castle Rock, Santa Barbara, Cal.

c. 1910

It was the culmination of Manifest Destiny. Americans trekked as far west as they possibly could. Invoking the name of the wrong explorer, Keats wrote, "Stout Cortez when with eagle eyes/He stared at the Pacific—and all his men/Looked at each other with a wild surmise." These pioneers and tourists could not have been more astonished when first they took a gander at the biggest ocean in the world. Inevitably, as the nineteenth century turned into the twentieth, each beach community—from Point Conception to the Mexican border—grew to reflect a separate facet of American life. What is one to make of this coast? Only that, like the rest of California, it is devoted equally to dreams of the rich and the poor and the pursuit of pleasure and of war.

Santa Barbara, the informal northern border of Southern California, represented all that was old, Republican, and very rich. Its inhabitants lived well and in perfect taste. Sophisticated couples sipped double martinis at the expensively constructed beach-side Biltmore, then cleared their heads by strolling along a manicured strand. Their diversions included women's clubs, historical societies, yachting, bathing, even hiking in the fragrant, chaparral-laden bluffs behind the city. The less affluent tourists might not have been able to afford the prices of the Hotel Arlington or the Potter or the Samarkand or the Biltmore, but they might visit the public bath house, stroll the seaside boulevards, or see the oldest woman tender in the cutest little lighthouse in California.

Just south of Santa Barbara, the towns of Ventura and Oxnard presented an entirely different aspect. People fished for a living. Vacationers camped modestly in tents by the shore. When you walked the beach in Ventura, you would come home with tar on your feet. Oil wells were everywhere, the odor of fish and sugar beets spiced the air. Ventura was a working man's home and haven. Here, in unspoiled territory, people lived simply, and confined their dreams to the necessities of life.

Then, for twenty miles, came a wilderness as pure and unspoiled as when Spanish explorers first saw it. Our federal government was responsible for that, snapping up that prime property, and using it now to train sailors on the fickle sea. Driving south, the tourist in his Model T slid past Malibu—territory of the stars—but would soon come upon signs of life—or at least hints of it—beginning where Topanga Canyon met the sea. This secluded wilderness traditionally housed outlaws—from the Spanish Vasquez, to bootleggers in the twenties, or colorful hippies in the sixties. Best to glance cautiously inland and drive on past rugged slopes carpeted in poppies and lupin. A few mansions of the very rich, like the Villa Leon, dotted this unspoiled Eden.

From the very beginning, the middle-class on vacation in Southern California flocked by the hundreds of thousands to Santa Monica, Ocean Park, and Venice. Convenient public transportation—Red Cars which had lines throughout the county—converged at this hospitable shore. Every twenty minutes those cars disgorged their eager cargo of sun-and-sea worshippers who dispersed across the sand in a happy frenzy. Here, packed in tighter than the proverbial sardines, people huddled under umbrellas of every stripe; they flung themselves with abandon into the shallow, inviting surf. They walked hand in hand along the cliff tops of Santa Monica—those treacherous, tricky bluffs that crumbled each week, each day, into the highway below, threatening unwary commuters.

Bathing in the Surf. Ocean Park, Cal.

c. 1910

Warf Scene, Redondo, Cal.

c. 1910

Santa Monica, Ocean Park, and Venice had everything. The Bristol Pier and the Concrete Pier are gone now, but part of the Pleasure Pier still stands, with one of the loveliest carrousels in the world. You could visit the "Camera Obscura" (sic) and see the world turned upside down. If this simple pleasure didn't satisfy you, you might dine in style at the Bristol Cafe or the Nat Goodwin or walk the exotic trails of Bernheimer's Chinese Gardens. The thrifty might rent a cabana for the day, taking the Red Car home, sunburned, sand-flecked, but happy; the well-off might stay at the Miramar or the Sovereign Hotel.

Down in Venice there was dancing, the miniature railway, and that last word in redundancy, the indoor pool at the Ocean Park Bath House. Venice was, in fact, one man's fantasy come true. Not content with the sequined Pacific, the scrubbed air, the exquisite cloudless skies, Abbot Kinney felt compelled to create a "Venice" echoing the original in Italy. At the turn of the century, Kinney, consumed by beneficent madness, dug a maze of canals through the brackish inland marshes; he crossed those canals with Venetian bridges and manned his gondolas with genuine Venetian gondoliers. He flanked Windward Avenue with Corinthian columns and arched loggias that (vaguely) recalled St. Mark's Square. The community flourished for a while, then, for decades, fell into disrepair. The fantasy was too "far out," even for Southern California. Today few canals remain, but Venice still prospers—the perfect Saturday afternoon treat. Where once tourists sedately strolled the strand, now that footpath is packed with slalom skateboarders, roller skaters, bicyclists, jugglers, fire-eaters, street-vendors, Rastafarians, pickpockets, Jewish senior citizens immortalized in film. If anything, Venice has surpassed Kinney's wildest surmise.

Every community has its romantic outposts. Depending on where you lived, Redondo, San Pedro, and Long Beach might fall into that category. Yes, there was a flagged pavilion, the turreted Hotel Redondo and of course the majestic hills of Palos Verdes. But these places were far out of town. Redondo was where raffish young men crowded to get in a little fishing and charming shop girls cavorted on the sandy beach. The sand was white, the water sparkling blue; but the glamor lay up north. San Pedro presented an alternate fantasy that might have sprung from the pages of Jack London or John Steinbeck. Brawny workers hefted lumber just down the shore or canned fish up on the inland hills. Shipbuilding may have produced income, but it also hinted of adventures yet to come. For years stern fathers warned their daughters away from Long Beach (even though it had been settled by Iowans). It was a Navy town and despite the sedate Villa Riviera, a girl could get into trouble between the sailors and the Long Beach Pike.

Nobody thought about trouble when it came to the Newport Peninsula and Balboa Island, however. That was where you went to have fun. Entire generations of California youth dated their first romances from Easter vacations spent in huge rented houses on the island and magic nights dancing in the Newport Pavilion. "The whole idea," recalls Carolyn See, California novelist, "was to stay in the sun until you turned green. But in spite of all that sunburn, romances were begun that lasted lifetimes." In the years before and during World War II, every big band in America came to play at Balboa and Newport. Sailors tossed their girls in the carefree movements of the New Yorker and the Lindy Hop.

Just south of all that came another citadel of the sedate and rich. Laguna Beach—a Bohemian hangout in the twenties—by the fifties conjured up the Victor Hugo Inn, old ladies with blue hair, painting and buying art of very dubious quality, strolling down to the Hotel Laguna for a change of pace (where now Ken Hansen of Scandia fame has turned this relic into a bastion of haute Swedish cuisine).

Oceanside told another story. It was a "service town, a military town." After the camouflaged tanks of Oceanside's maneuvers, what could be

3020 – Happy Youngsters on the Beach.

c. 1910

Yachting on the Pacific.

M. Rieder, Publ. Los Angeles, Cal. 8025. Made in Germany

c. 1905

more "Californian" than the luxurious cliffs of La Jolla where the tennis club glistens like egg shells in the sunlight and—far from any postcard—Dr. Suess lives in lordly splendor and puts gold flatware on his luncheon table? And once past La Jolla, what could be more natural than to arrive at one of America's largest naval bases? For years, and especially during World War II, San Diego was home to hundreds of ships and thousands of sailors. Their young wives followed the fleet and settled in this lovely town, contenting themselves with pleasing diversions—trying their luck at the amusement center at Mission Beach, picnicking in Balboa Park, rambling along Sunset Cliffs, dressing up for dates at the El Cortez Sky Room for a "never to be forgotten view," and perhaps seeking spiritual enlightenment at the Theosophical Institute at Point Loma. Many of these Navy families who had left their landbound homes to see the world were loath to return. They would make San Diego their home after the war. For a special occasion they might take the ferry across the bay to the Hotel Del Coronado, where every eligible debutante once claimed to have danced with the Prince of Wales on his first world tour. Then came the border and the mystery of Mexico.

If all this were not enough, the beach of all beaches was "Twenty Six Miles Across the Sea," a perfect jewel of the Pacific, Catalina Island. The Wrigleys of chewing gum fame purchased most of it, but the town of Avalon remained for the simple folk and was a source of perpetual enjoyment. You could go for the day on the S.S. Catalina where a recorded loudspeaker met you with the strains of "Avalon," crane your head toward the aquatic wonders underneath the glass bottom boat, or take other boats at night to spy the flying fish. You could walk down to the Casino where gambling was forbidden but the ceiling of the ballroom had twinkling lights for stars. Through the years, big wooden hotels were built and then burned, built and then burned, but the island—like all of this seductive coast—continued to exert its charm.

SB.65   LOS CRUCES CREEK, ENTRANCE TO GAVIOTA PASS, NEAR SANTA BARBARA, CALIFORNIA

c. 1920

Bay of Santa Barbara, Cal.

c. 1910

998 – STREET SCENE, SANTA BARBARA, CALIFORNIA.

c. 1910

Originally a mission pueblo, Santa Barbara early attracted vacationers and residents to its bay. An earthquake leveled many of its buildings on June 29, 1925, and the city center was rebuilt as a planned unit in the mission style of architecture.

"EL PASEO DE LA GUERRA", SANTA BARBARA, CALIFORNIA

3A-H591

c. 1935

SANTA BARBARA COUNTY COURT HOUSE, SANTA BARBARA, CALIFORNIA

3A-H604

c. 1940

A Santa Barbara Home on Hill back of Bath House, Santa Barbara, Cal.

c. 1910

SB-75—Coral Casino Swimming Pool, Santa Barbara Biltmore, Santa Barbara, California

OB-H2650

c. 1940

2636 – POTTER COUNTRY CLUB, HOPE RANCH, SANTA BARBARA, CALIFORNIA.

c. 1910

SB-92   THE SAMARKAND, PERSIAN HOTEL, SANTA BARBARA, CALIFORNIA

c. 1925

2213 – Hotel Potter, Santa Barbara, California.   Road of a Thousand Wonders.

c. 1910

SB-54.   SEASIDE BOULEVARD, SANTA BARBARA, CALIF.

c. 1920

3332 – California's largest Rose Bush. Santa Barbara, Cal.

c. 1905

More than one community claimed its own "biggest" and "largest," but the "oldest" lady lighthouse keeper was unique— and this rosebush withstood all challengers.

The Light House and Oldest Woman Tender in the U. S. near Santa Barbara, Cal.

c. 1910

The Largest Grape Vine in the World. 9 ft. in circumference, Carpinteria near Santa Barbara, Cal.

c. 1910

CHAUTAUQUA GROUNDS, VENTURA, CAL.

c. 1925

SB-101   CAUSEWAY, COAST HIGHWAY, BETWEEN VENTURA AND SANTA BARBARA, CALIFORNIA

117430

c. 1925

Ventura, Cal., in 1875.

c. 1910

13178   MATILIJA STAGE COACH, VENTURA CO., CALIF.

c. 1925

873 - WHARF AT VENTURA, CALIFORNIA

DWARD H. MITCHELL, PUBLISHER, SAN FRANCISCO.

c. 1905

70931 A DAY'S CATCH IN VENTURA COUNTY, CALIF.

c. 1920

HOTEL VENTURA, VENTURA, CALIFORNIA

ONE OF LEADING AND NEWEST HOTELS, BETWEEN SAN FRANCISCO AND LOS ANGELES

c. 1920

The Sugar Factory, Oxnard, Cal.

c. 1910

317:—Beach Road and Entrance to Topanga Canyon, near Santa Monica, Calif.

c. 1920

SM-41   PALATIAL HOME AND MALIBU SHORELINE, ROOSEVELT HIGHWAY, NEAR SANTA MONICA, CALIFORNIA

c. 1920

S. M. 8.   Along the Palisades, Santa Monica, California.

c. 1920

OVERLOOKING THE OCEAN FROM THE PALISADES, SANTA MONICA, CALIF.

c. 1910

SM-37—Beach Homes of the Stars along the Palisades, Santa Monica, California

c. 1940

M. 2, SANTA MONICA CANYON, SANTA MONICA, CALIFORNIA.

c. 1910

In July 1875, Senator John P. Jones and Colonel R. S. Baker bought the Spanish landgrants and sold lots to the new city of Santa Monica. The auctioneer promised buyers a daily sunset of "scarlet and gold" and "a bay filled with white-winged ships." He added that the land was guaranteed by his employers, but the title to "the ocean, the sunset, and the air . . . by God."

c. 1910

c. 1925

The Bristol Cafe, Santa Monica, Cal.

c. 1910

SM-15.   PLEASURE PIER, SANTA MONICA, CALIFORNIA.

c. 1925

6804.   Bristol Pier, Santa Monica, California.

c. 1910

A CARLOAD OF BATHING BEAUTIES SANTA MONICA, CAL.   F-161

c. 1925

FAMOUS CAMERA OBSCURA, SANTA MONICA, CALIF.

c. 1910

SM-16—Daily Scene on the Beach at Santa Monica, California

PHOTO BY "DICK" WHITTINGTON   1B-H2163

c. 1945

c. 1920

MIRAMAR HOTEL & BUNGALOWS • SANTA MONICA, CALIFORNIA

c. 1940

803 – Beach and Roller Coaster, Ocean Park, California.

c. 1910

2409 – Broad Walk between Venice and Ocean Park, California.

c. 1910

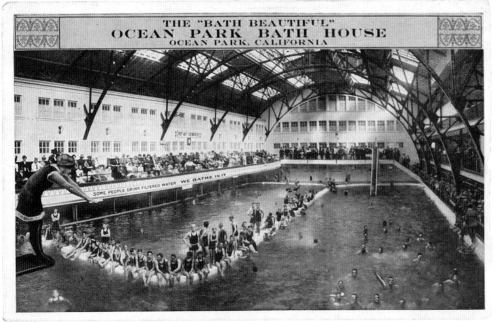

THE "BATH BEAUTIFUL"
OCEAN PARK BATH HOUSE
OCEAN PARK, CALIFORNIA

c. 1920

2882 – Ocean Front, Looking South, Ocean Park, California.

c. 1910

Daily Scene on the Salt Water Canals, Venice, Cal.

c. 1910

Venice High School, Venice, California.

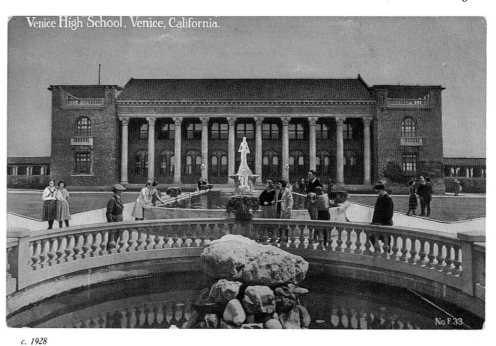

c. 1928

The Miniature Railway, Venice, Cal.

c. 1910

c. 1910

V-26. Boating on the Canal, Venice, California.

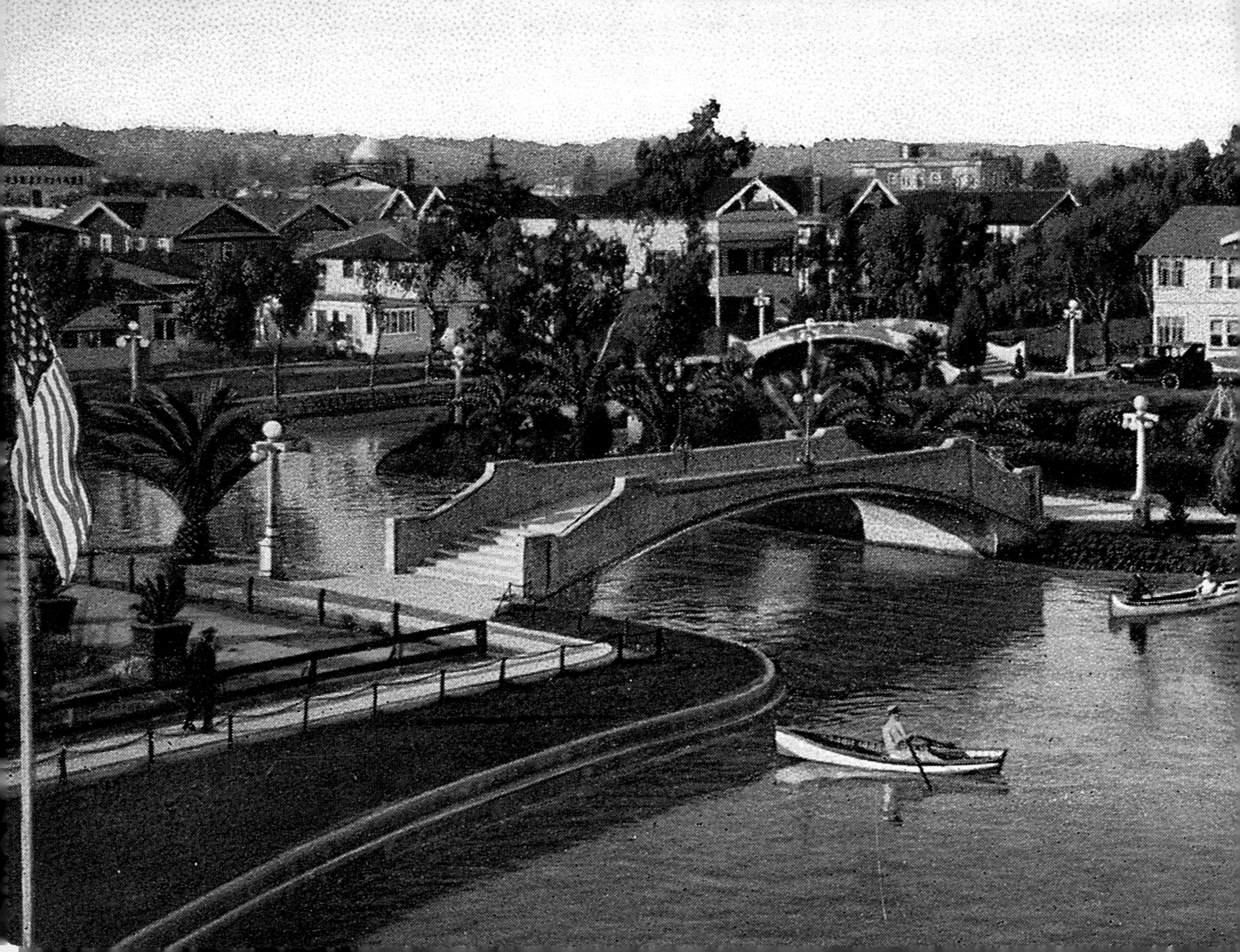

The Colonnade, Windward Ave., Venice, Cal.

c. 1910

Fun on the Beach, Venice, Cal.

c. 1910

A CROWDED DAY AT VENICE, CALIFORNIA   T237

c. 1925

BEACH SCENE, VENICE, CALIFORNIA   F-22

c. 1925

c. 1910

2801 Hunting for Moonstones on the Beach at Redondo, California

c. 1910

MUNICIPAL PIER, MANHATTAN BEACH, CALIFORNIA—13

c. 1940

HOTEL REDONDO, REDONDO BEACH, CALIFORNIA.

c. 1920

586 View from the Palo Verde Hills, California, Redondo Beach and Hermosa Beach in the Distance

8A-H3004

c. 1940

200:—U. S. BATTLESHIPS ANCHORED AT LONG BEACH, CALIFORNIA.

c. 1945

Greetings FROM CALIFORNIA

201:—SKYLINE, LONG BEACH, CALIFORNIA.

c. 1945

Greetings from LONG BEACH CALIFORNIA

c. 1945

Many of the original Long Beach buildings were destroyed on March 10, 1933, when an earthquake leveled parts of the city. Luckily, the quake occurred on a weekend, so the many school buildings that suffered were empty. For days after the initial temblor, many residents camped out in tent cities until the aftershocks had subsided.

Front Street at San Pedro Harbor, Los Angeles, Cal.

c. 1910

500 Ship Building at Los Angeles Harbor, San Pedro, Cal.

c. 1910

A center of maritime repair and shipbuilding from its earliest days, the community of San Pedro reached its peak in these industries during World War II.

Unloading Lumber, San Pedro, California.

c. 1920

c. 1910

Fishing Scene near Los Angeles, Cal.

1010 — SUNSET ON THE BEACH.

SHELTERED BATHING BEACH AND FAMOUS "PAGODA" HOUSE,
ENTRANCE TO NEWPORT HARBOR, CALIFORNIA—46

c. 1945

ANCHORAGE OF NEWPORT HARBOR YACHT CLUB, NEWPORT HARBOR, CALIFORNIA—42

c. 1945

*Victor Hugo Inn and Heisler Park Floral Gardens,
Laguna Beach, California*

PHOTO BY R. NOBLE ESTEY

4B-H419

c. 1945

c. 1910

Hotel Laguna, Laguna Beach, California

HOTEL LAGUNA

c. 1945

LA JOLLA BEACH AND TENNIS CLUB, LA JOLLA, CALIF.—142

c. 1940

3812 Sphinx Head Cave, La Jolla, San Diego, California

c. 1910

The Indians first called the area *la hoya*, meaning "the cave," later changed to a local spelling of *La Joya*, "the jewel."

Sand-Witches on the Beach.

c. 1920

c. 1910

c. 1910

c. 1905

FIFTH AVE. AUTO WASH, FIFTH AND KALMIA, SAN DIEGO, CALIF.

c. 1920

One of the many Flower Gardens under the individual care of San Diego School Children, San Diego, Cal.

c. 1915

4547—Santa Fe Station, San Diego, California

c. 1940

4254. U. S. Grant Hotel, San Diego, Cal.

c. 1915

4546—PBY Plane in Flight over San Diego, California

1B-H1010

c. 1940

4241. Pacific Torpedo Fleet, San Diego, Cal.

c. 1915

824N   BEDDING INSPECTION. U. S. NAVAL TRAINING STATION. SAN DIEGO, CALIFORNIA

E-4173

c. 1940

T319   MUNICIPAL PIER. SAN DIEGO, CALIFORNIA

c. 1940

c. 1945

After World War II, many of America's intrepid men of the sea and their faithful wives decided to make the city of San Diego their permanent home. This sunny metropolis, one wife confided to her parents, was "the prettiest place I've ever seen."

DRINKING IN THE SKY . . . a never-to-be forgotten view · EL CORTEZ SKY ROOM, San Diego, California

c. 1950

c. 1945

MISSION BEACH, CALIFORNIA—36

c. 1945

AMUSEMENT CENTER, MISSION BEACH, SAN DIEGO, CALIF.—145

GIANT DIPPER

MALTS

c. 1945

SAN DIEGO AND CORONADO FERRY, SAN DIEGO, CALIFORNIA—80

c. 1945

Once the Coronado Bridge had been built, the ferry went out of service, but in 1987, the ride in its ineffable beauty was brought back—by popular demand.

HOTEL DEL CORONADO, ACROSS THE BAY FROM
SAN DIEGO, CALIFORNIA

c. 1910

The Dining Room, Coronado Hotel, Coronado, Cal.

c. 1910

4330. The Beach, Tent City, Coronado, Cal.

c. 1910

Sea Wall and Boulevard, Coronado, Cal.

c. 1910

c. 1910

North Island, Coronado and San Diego,
California from an Aeroplane.

Avalon, Santa Catalina Island, Cal.

Bath House, Catalina Island, Cal.

c. 1910

15151. Catalina Island Tuna Club, Avalon, Catalina Island.

c. 1910

c. 1910

Sword Fish caught at Santa Catalina Island, Cal., weight 292 lbs, time 25 minutes.

c. 1910

Owned by chewing gum magnate William Wrigley, Catalina Island lured Dr. Charles Frederick Holder, who delighted in having his picture taken with fish that were bigger than he was. In 1898, he founded the Tuna Club, that exists to this day.

C-18   A Glimpse of the Yacht Club and Casino, Santa Catalina Island, California

c. 1940

C-90—The Beach in Front of Hotel St. Catherine, Santa Catalina, California

c. 1940

C-40—Former Residence of Zane Grey, Avalon, Santa Catalina, California

c. 1940

STEAMER CATALINA ARRIVING AT AVALON CATALINA ISLAND, CAL   J-36

c. 1925

3119 - Boys Diving for Coins, Avalon, Catalina Island, California.

c. 1910

Sugar Loaf & Glass Bottom Boats at Santa Catalina Island, Cal.

c. 1910

11499 VIEWING THE MARINE GARDENS, SANTA CATALINA ISLAND, CALIF.

c. 1920

In 1888, glass bottom boats began treating ordinarily earthbound tourists to sightings of the elusive garibaldi, trigger fish, lobster, opal-eye, kelp fish, and godi.

The Real L.A.

GREETINGS FROM LOS ANGELES

2199 – A CALIFORNIA HONEYMOON
COPYRIGHT 1910 BY EDWARD H. MITCHELL SAN FRANCISCO

c. 1910

When English novelist Christopher Isherwood first came to Los Angeles, he protested to his friends back home that there was no way any description could encompass all of L.A. Then he went on to characterize Sunset Boulevard a few miles west of Downtown as a charming valley bounded by parched hills, etched along the top with "palm trees like lace." When French essayist Jacques Barzun undertook to describe the same metropolis, he too chose Sunset going westward toward the sea: to him, it seemed more beautiful than the Riviera's Grande Corniche. Other visitors railed at L.A, however. There was no center, they said; no Downtown. One of them dismissed the amorphous community set precariously between desert and ocean as "six suburbs in search of a city." Others dismissed it as a state of mind.

In truth, Los Angeles is primarily a state of mind. Its "Downtown" began on the banks of the sluggish Los Angeles River next to a Spanish settlement called the City of the Angeles. (Olvera Street, a scant mile from this early settlement, salutes this Latin past.) But "Downtown" moved westward quickly, into Hollywood, the Miracle Mile, Beverly Hills, Westwood, and so on. L.A. is a town without a center, without borders, and proud of it.

The city fathers did the right thing by Downtown, but their best monuments seemed mostly dedicated to pleasures. The early years of this century saw a plethora of floral displays: the Bernheimer Gardens, the Japanese Tea Gardens, and the Busch Gardens. Even Forest Lawn, the world's gaudiest cemetery where "we landscape our dead," was one big flower and sculpture garden.

When Los Angeles successfully bid for the 1932 Olympic Games, it built the Coliseum, large enough, boosters bragged, to hold the whole population of the state of Nevada. Characteristically, they flanked that stadium with the Exposition Park Rose Garden. Elsewhere, the Hollywood Bowl lay in a fragrant natural canyon. Elysian Park would later be known as the neighbor of Dodger Stadium, but at that time it housed—and still does—a T.B. sanatorium in a rural setting where recovery was virtually assured.

If you asked the occupants of any given six suburbs—for example, Glendale, Pasadena, Altadena, Highland Park, Santa Monica, Culver City—where the "center" of the metropolis lay, they'd probably put their feet down where they were and say, "Right here." Pasadena, in particular, called itself "the crown city" of the San Gabriel Valley. And after World War II, when our boys came home in search of bungalows big enough for two, or three or four or more, they moved into yet another unspoiled "wilderness," the San Fernando Valley. Literally millions would settle there, building their versions of the Southern California dream. If, in time, they would do their best to "turn paradise into a parking lot," paradise would defeat their plans. To see the valley from Mulholland Drive even now is to look upon an ocean of green.

Downtown? The center? It might be Angel's Flight or, if you worked in the movies, the Beverly Hills Hotel, or, if you were the conservative type just in the from the East, a tree-lined street in Pasadena. What did it matter where the center was? The trick was to go to Westlake Park or Eastlake Park or whatever park took your fancy, row out to the middle of the lake, and let your fingers trail in the water. You were home. You were in L.A.

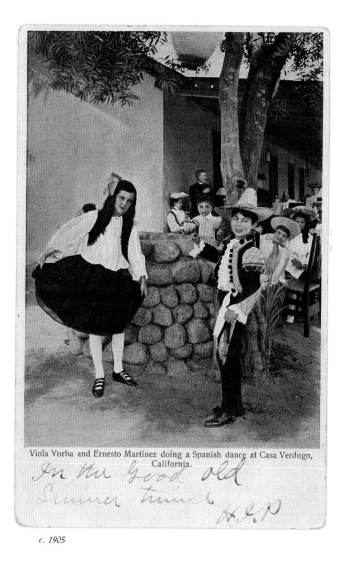

Viola Vorba and Ernesto Martinez doing a Spanish dance at Casa Verdugo, California.

In the Good old Summer time H.C.P

c. 1905

872—The Original Farmers Market, Hollywood, California

PHOTO BY "DICK" WHITTINGTON

1B-H215Z

c. 1945

611—PUBLIC LIBRARY, LOS ANGELES, CALIFORNIA

c. 1945

607 BROWN DERBY RESTAURANT, LOS ANGELES, CALIFORNIA

c. 1945

LA-74—Busy Crowds on Wilshire Boulevard, Los Angeles, California

PHOTO BY "DICK" WHITTINGTON

1B-H2147

c. 1945

LA. 25—New Union Station, Los Angeles, California

9A-H637

c. 1935

612 THE CITY HALL AND THE STEPHEN M. WHITE STATUE.

LOS ANGELES, CALIFORNIA

c. 1940

LA-29—Waiting Room, Union Station, Los Angeles, California

9A-H918

c. 1935

El Pueblo de Nuestra Señora La Reyna de Los Angeles de la Porciúncula was founded in December 1781 by forty-four somewhat reluctant colonists of mixed race from Mexico. In time, the city's name was shortened to Los Angeles, L.A.

Main Street near Third, Los Angeles, Cal.

c. 1910

Angel's Flight and Elk Building, Los Angeles, Cal.

c. 1910

When Angel's Flight, at Third and Hill streets, opened on New Year's Eve, 1901, passengers were given a free ride and a cup of fruit punch. Angel's Flight was dismantled in 1969, and plans are still pending to reconstruct it.

BOSTON SHOE MARKET INC. ENTIRE 4TH FLOOR, ORPHEUM BUILDING, 636 SO. BROADWAY, LOS ANGELES, CALIF.

c. 1910

LA-19   TYPICAL OF EARLY LOS ANGELES—OLVERA STREET, LOS ANGELES, CALIFORNIA

6A-H2613

c. 1940

LA-66—Plaza in China City, Los Angeles, California

PHOTO BY "DICK" WHITTINGTON

QB-H2593

c. 1940

41:-NEW CHINATOWN, LOS ANGELES, CALIFORNIA

罗致菁华

LOOKING EAST ALONG GIN LING WAY

47508

c. 1940

Sing Fat Co. Inc.
Kimona Section, So. Broadway at
6th St. Hill St. at 6th St. Los Angeles, Cal.

c. 1910

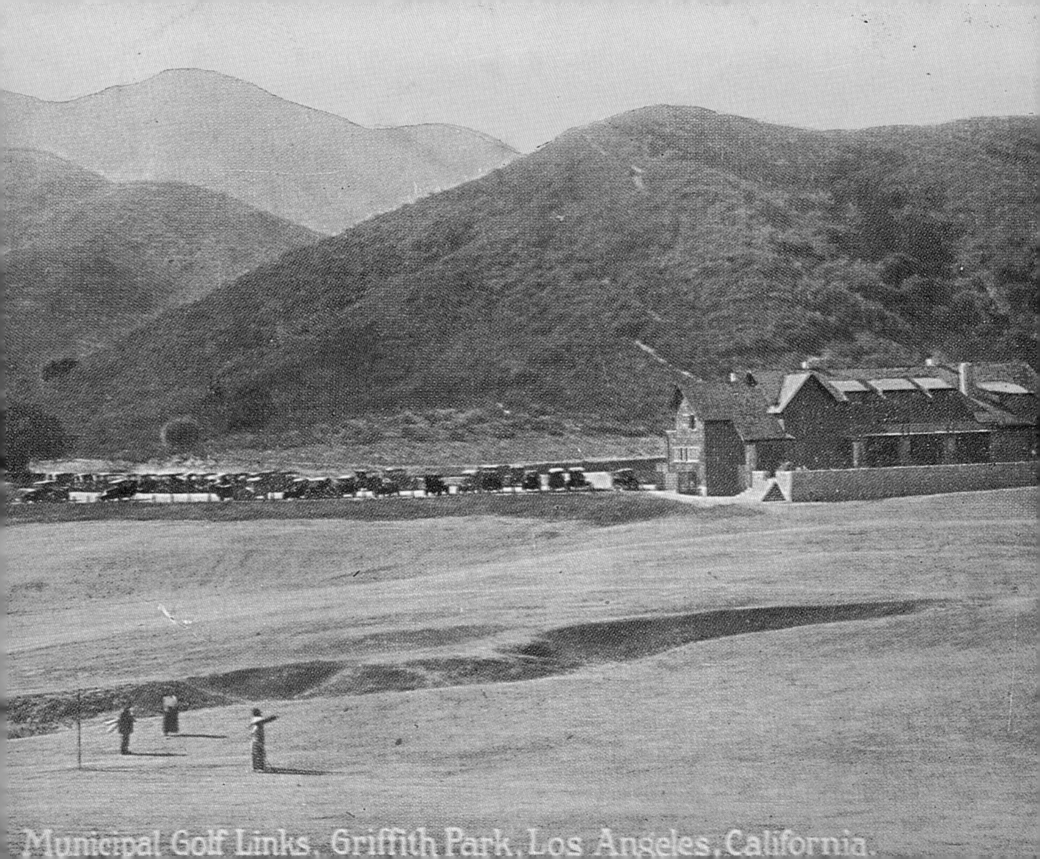

Municipal Golf Links, Griffith Park, Los Angeles, California.

BAND STAND AND BOAT HOUSE,
EAST LAKE PARK, LOS ANGELES, CAL. 9803

c. 1910

Winter in Eastlake Park,
Los Angeles, California.

c. 1910

c. 1915

9793 A WINTER SCENE, WEST LAKE PARK, LOS ANGELES, CAL.

c. 1910

"We used to fish for carp in Westlake Park. We rolled bread into balls for bait and sometimes caught fifteen-pounders, which we sold. On a good day we made enough for popcorn, crackerjack, and, by pooling our money, an hour's rowboat ride." (Matt Weinstock, *My L.A.*) Westlake Park, which was created in 1885, was renamed MacArthur Park in 1942.

c. 1915

c. 1915

Aimee Semple McPherson, founder of the Four Square Gospel Church, put on extravagant religious ceremonies at the Angelus Temple during the twenties and thirties. She once began a service by tearing up to the pulpit on a motorcycle.

c. 1920

c. 1910

Hotel Hollywood Court, Hollywood, California

c. 1910

Lobby, Hotel Alexandria, Los Angeles, Cal.

70513 HOTEL ALEXANDRIA, LOS ANGELES, CALIF.

c. 1910

c. 1910

Beverly Hills Hotel, Beverly Hills, Cal.

c. 1910

BEVERLY-WILSHIRE HOTEL, BEVERLY HILLS, CALIFORNIA   T 271

c. 1920

A glimpse of the Beverly Hills Hotel, Beverly Hills, California.

c. 1910

MIDWAY BETWEEN LOS ANGELES AND THE SEA. OPEN ALL THE YEAR.

CHOIR BOYS, SUNDAY MORNING, BEVERLY HILLS HOTEL AND BUNGALOWS, BEVERLY HILLS, CALIFORNIA

c. 1920

One of Los Angeles' Fine Homes

c. 1910

A Modern California Adobe Home.

c. 1910

PRACTICAL BUNGALOWS

JUST OUT—1912 Edition of "PRACTICAL BUNGALOWS." About 60 one and two-story bungalows suited to any climate, nearly 170 illustrations, exterior interiors and plan plates. Building hints and cost prices. Issued by Largest Co-operative Building Company in the World. Most practical bungalow book published. Sent post paid for 50 Cents in P.O. order, stamps or coin. Money back if not worth double the price.
LOS ANGELES INVESTMENT COMPANY
Third and Hill Streets, Los Angeles, Cal.

50 CENTS   BUILT BY   LOS ANGELES INVESTMENT COMPANY   1912 EDITION

c. 1912

Residence at Los Angeles, Cal.

c. 1910

Japanese Garden of a California Home.

c. 1910

The Entrance to a California Home.
Girls Collegiate School, Los Angeles.

c. 1905

Traditionally, Americans with green thumbs took Old Man Winter into account. In Southern California, instead of being content with a potted geranium in the kitchen window, they could let their gardens—and imaginations—run wild.

A Typical Rose Covered Adobe Home, California.

c. 1910

c. 1910

Main Street of Culver City, Los Angeles, Cal.

BEL AIR COUNTRY CLUB, WESTWOOD HILLS, LOS ANGELES, CALIFORNIA   LA17

846.   MULHOLLAND DRIVE, SANTA MONICA MOUNTAINS, NEAR HOLLYWOOD, CALIFORNIA.

c. 1920

c. 1920

104183

LA-117—Coliseum, Exposition Park, Los Angeles, California

838   UNIVERSITY OF CALIFORNIA AT LOS ANGELES, WESTWOOD HILLS, CALIFORNIA

1B-H140

5A-H367

c. 1940

c. 1940

c. 1940

c. 1920

George N. Laws, noted collector, has observed that the automobile began to appear in California postcards between 1908 and 1910. But by 1915, Los Angeles had established its world record for automobile ownership with 55,217 cars.

c. 1910

c. 1910

406:—SANTA ANITA RACE TRACK, ARCADIA, CALIFORNIA.

CLUB HOUSE AND GRAND STAND, LOS ANGELES TURF CLUB.   45057

c. 1940

877--Easter Sunrise Services, Hollywood Bowl, Hollywood, California

7B·H2074

c. 1940

188 *The Mystery of Life, Forest Lawn Memorial Park, Glendale, California*

FOREST LAWN
MEMORIAL PARK

THE   MYSTERY   OF   LIFE

7A-H3617

c. 1940

In 1917, Forest Lawn was founded by Dr. Hubert L. Eaton, who thought of his cemetery as "a great park, devoid of misshapen monuments where lovers new and old shall love to stroll." Eaton's major contribution to contemporary art remains an astonishing number of marble fig leaves.

P-44 THE HUNTINGTON MEMORIAL LIBRARY, SAN MARINO, NEAR PASADENA, CALIFORNIA

123318

c. 1920

Arroyo Seco, Colorado Street Bridge, Pasadena, Cal.

c. 1915

View of the Busch Sunken Gardens, Pasadena, Cal.

c. 1910

The Lake Ave. Methodist Church, Pasadena, Cal.

c. 1910

III – Gardens of Hotel Green, Pasadena, California.

c. 1910

6192. RAYMOND HOTEL, PASADENA, CAL. COPYRIGHT 1902, BY DETROIT PHOTOGRAPHIC CO.

c. 1902

2741 – A Walk Beneath the Pepper Trees in Beautiful California.

c. 1910

Affluent vacationers in Pasadena had a choice of several hostelries: the Green, Huntington, Vista Del Arroyo, and Raymond. In 1887, the newly-completed Raymond Hotel burned to the ground. It was rebuilt and then reopened in 1901.

Hollywoodland

THE LATE RUDOLPH VALENTINO MOUNTED ON JADAAN

c. 1935

In the teens of this century, the movie industry back east was having a terrible time of it. Hopeful, moviemakers came west. Los Angeles at that time was still centered around the Plaza. It took a twenty-minute ride on the Red Car to get out to the hamlet of Hollywood.

Once there, it was an everyday occurrence to see movies being shot in the streets. Mack Sennett staged improbable car chases with his Keystone Cops, Buster Keaton tempted death, and Cecil B. De Mille's first studio occupied an unpretentious barn. The industry seemed a wholesome, low-budget pastime. These cinematic gypsies used the sun to light their sets and waited for disasters so that they might film a disaster movie. But overnight, this pastime became big business.

Walled studios sprang up, rendering moviemaking inaccessible to tourists. The public saw only a carefully constructed exterior: "Movie star homes" seen from the cramped confines of a tourist bus. Never mind that the real Hollywood was somewhere else.

In the evenings at a premiere, fans might crowd against police cordons, jostling for a sight of their favorite celebrity. If these film stars made up the new American royalty, surely the magnificent first-run movie theaters of Hollywood were their palaces. The Egyptian required of its audiences a block-long walk in the fanciful environs of ancient Egypt before they could reach their seats. But Grauman's Chinese offered even more: the foot- and handprints of the stars.

Buster Keaton in one of his comedies, Hollywood.

c. 1920

"Faking" a Snow Scene in Tropical California, Mack Sennett Studios, Edendale.

c. 1920

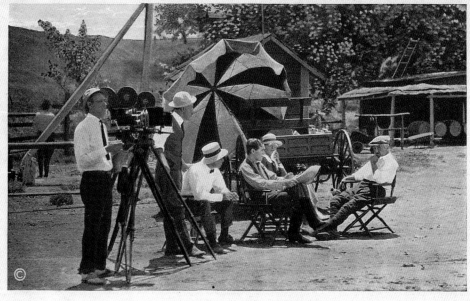

Charles Ray and Staff, The Charles Ray Productions, Hollywood.

c. 1920

303:—MARION DAVIES AND HER COLONIAL BEACH HOME, SANTA MONICA, CALIF.

c. 1920

Visitors' Observation Platform, Universal City, California

c. 1910

FOX STUDIOS AT WESTWOOD, CALIF.   A-97

c. 1925

PARAMOUNT FAMOUS LASKY STUDIO, HOLLYWOOD, CALIF.   A-94

c. 1925

802:—Willat Studio, Washington Blvd., near Los Angeles, Cal.

c. 1920

856—Columbia Square, Home of KNX Columbia Broadcasting System, Hollywood, California

c. 1940

National Broadcasting Station, Radio City, Hollywood, Calif.

c. 1940

835— American Broadcasting Company (KECA), Vine Street, Hollywood, California

c. 1940

These pre-World War II network buildings are seen by us as television studios today. But then, radio ruled. Fibber McGee and Molly, George Burns and Gracie Allen, Jack Benny, Fred Allen, and even the Lone Ranger all plied their trade, during the thirties and for a last few magic years before television won the great media battles for the hearts and minds of America.

c. 1940

c. 1930

In 1919, Mary Pickford and Douglas Fairbanks, long Hollywood's happiest married couple, constructed this "cottage-style" mansion. These two, along with Charlie Chaplin, first broke away from the studio system to form their own corporation, United Artists. This prompted a disgruntled executive to remark, "The inmates have taken over the asylum."

c. 1925

817—Residence of Myrna Loy, near Beverly Hills, California

OB-H510

c. 1945

802   HOME OF BING CROSBY, TOLUCA LAKE, NORTH HOLLYWOOD, CALIF.

c. 1945

819—Beach Home of Cary Grant, Santa Monica, California

1B-H1017

c. 1945

834—Residence of Dorothy Lamour, Beverly Hills, California

OB-H508

c. 1945

824   HOLLYWOODLAND, BEAUTIFUL RESIDENTIAL DISTRICT

IN THE HILLS OF HOLLYWOOD, CALIFORNIA

643-29

c. 1925

813.   "THE HOUSE THAT JOKES BUILT", HOME OF WILL ROGERS, BEVERLY HILLS, CALIFORNIA.

c. 1925

801   HOLLYWOOD BOULEVARD, HOLLYWOOD, CALIFORNIA

646-29

c. 1925

HENRY'S CAFE, HOLLYWOOD, CALIFORNIA

c. 1925

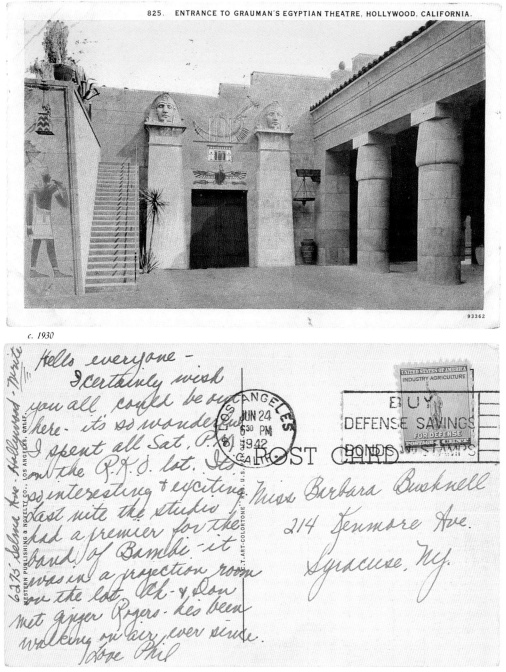

c. 1930

c. 1940

c. 1940

Impresario Sid Grauman opened the Egyptian in 1926. Two years later, he would improve on "perfection" with his pseudo-Oriental masterpiece, Grauman's Chinese.

Beyond Boundaries

R-39—Highway Bridge across Santa Ana River, Riverside, California

A Picturesque Highway in California

c. 1940

Where does the city of Los Angeles end? The truth is, there are no boundaries. It's indicative of the amorphous quality of some of these Southern California cities that they don't lend themselves to generalization. Now they are called the Inland Empire. When they began, each of them represented a particular manifestation of a point of view, a way of life. Originally, the interior valleys, such as the San Gabriel, held independent settlements: Upland, peopled by a group of utopian idealists; Santa Ana and Anaheim, by German immigrants; Redlands, by Baptists; Riverside by prosperous Englishmen; and San Bernardino—at the end of the Mormon Trail—by Latter-day Saints who hoped to extend their spiritual influence. Though traces of these origins remain, today the communities tend to merge.

Inland, separate from the city, these pioneers created or discovered their own resorts, and many of them had to do with the ubiquitous pursuit of health. The Indians had cured themselves in hot springs, and the newcomers did likewise, soaking at Glen Ivy, Murietta, Wheeler, or Urbita in mud, tule roots, or pungent sulfuric baths. The San Bernardino Mountains offered Lake Arrowhead and Big Bear, both man-made bodies of water, where in high, cool mountain air, vacationers could take their ease. The lakes teemed with croppie and bluegill; weekend sportsmen might pull in enough in one afternoon to feed their ravenous families who enthusiastically played at living outdoors, bringing Huck Finn fantasies to this tamed western landscape.

A Business Street in Pomona, Cal.

c. 1910

Hotel Ontario, Ontario, Cal.

c. 1910

Rapid Transit in Ontario, Calif. In 1895.

ONTARIO & SAN ANTONIO HEIGHTS R.R. CO.

c. 1910

VISITORS BEING ENTERTAINED AT STABLES ON W. K. KELLOGG ARABIAN HORSE RANCH, POMONA, CALIF.

c. 1925

Looking West on Center Street, Anaheim, Cal.

c. 1915

2939 – Fourth Street, Santa Ana, California.

c. 1915

As orchards and groves grew and flourished to the south of Los Angeles, Orange County developed its own independent commercial centers and transportation systems.

Walnut Grove, Fullerton, Cal.

c. 1915

c. 1905

San Gabriel on a Busy Day.

Palm Drive.
Uplands, Cal.

c. 1910

IN FRONT OF LOBBY AT GILMAN'S RELIEF HOT SPRINGS, SAN JACINTO, CALIF.

c. 1915

Hot springs have always attracted seekers after health and social contacts. Early southern Californians followed the lead of native Indians in visiting springs that were later developed into resorts, each with its devoted clientele.

c. 1920

Sherman Institute, Indian School, Riverside, Calif.

c. 1915

13353 CAJON ST. SHOWING FOUR CHURCHES, REDLANDS, CAL.

c. 1925

COPR. DETROIT PUBLISHING CO.

13350 BASIN AND PERGOLA, KIMBERLY CREST, REDLANDS, CAL.

c. 1925

San Timeteo Canyon from Smiley Heights
Redlands, Cal.

c. 1915

The Old Bell, Rubidoux Mt., Riverside, Cal.

c. 1910

R.57   ROTUNDA WING, MISSION INN, RIVERSIDE, CALIFORNIA

2A-H135

c. 1940

In 1902, when Frank Miller constructed his astonishing Mission Inn in Riverside, he said that he didn't care if they never sold one drink in the bar, if he could bring people to the beauty of the ages, the Inn as a way of life. His imaginative displays included a set of catacombs, a St. Francis of Assisi Chapel and wax effigies of the Papal Court of Pius X.

79420 CLOISTER MUSIC ROOM - GLENWOOD MISSION INN, RIVERSIDE, CALIFORNIA.   COPR. DETROIT PUBLISHING CO.

c. 1915

c. 1915

Mt. San Bernardino from Redlands, Cal.

The Stewart Hotel, San Bernardino, Cal.

c. 1910

2454 – THIRD STREET AND MT. SAN BERNARDINO, SAN BERNARDINO, CALIFORNIA.

c. 1910

1512 – CITY WELL, SAN BERNARDINO, CALIFORNIA.

c. 1910

B-20   Big Bear Lake, California

On the "Rim o' the World Drive" in the San Bernardino Mountains

c. 1940

Arrowhead Hot Springs Hotel, Arrowhead Springs, Cal.

c. 1925

LAKE ARROWHEAD IN ARROWHEAD WOODS, CALIFORNIA.

A-03.   THE JOY OF LIVING.   88866

c. 1925

LAKE ARROWHEAD IN ARROWHEAD WOODS, CALIFORNIA

B-929   THE BATHING COVE   2A508

c. 1925

Lake Arrowhead offered a pleasing contrast to the bustling city of Los Angeles. Here, tourists might forget their troubles and return to scenery that, with its greenery and occasional snow, reminded them of old days—old ways.

110° In The Shade

DEATH VALLEY NATIONAL MONUMENT, CALIFORNIA

© FRASHERS PHOTO   "THE DEVIL'S CORN FIELD"   3A-H1534

c. 1940

In order to get to Los Angeles, travelers from the east had to cross the Mojave Desert. That desert is always present, even in the city, even in its resorts. Every year, scorching Santa Ana winds, whipping down the canyons out of the blistering Mojave, sweep through the city.

In the city it was easy to forget that the desert was all around. But as with the coast, it encompassed every aspect of society. In Palm Springs, a hundred miles due east of Los Angeles, the rich cavorted, creating complex Hollywood sandcastles. Farther down the road, Indio offered an old-fashioned oasis chock-full of succulent dates. But up over the Cajon Pass, what people still call the High Desert attracted visionaries. Many of them had originally come by train and had fallen in love with the austere magnificence of the desert landscape. Stopping at Needles to take on water just over the California border, travelers might safely play the tourist role, purchasing curios from peaceful and courteous Indians. They fell in love with the wild west challenge of Barstow or Victorville where the earth is flat as a pancake and hot as a griddle. Cowboy star Roy Rogers was so enamored of the ambiance that he created a resort in its midst, Apple Valley, which has endured to this year.

The desert is full of secrets and people with secrets. It's for those who love the sidewinders, the coyotes, and the electric orchid of the sun as it bursts forth in the morning, tinting the whole world for a few precious seconds an ineffable and mysterious lavender. . . .

El Portal Apt. Hotel - PALM SPRINGS, CALIF.

1563 No. Palm Canyon Drive - Phone: 9053

c. 1950

This Natural Hot Mineral Water Pool is maintained at about 95 degrees with a constant flow of approximately 125 gallons a minute.

c. 1950

Historic INDIAN WELLS MOTEL AND TRAILER PARK

INDIO, CALIFORNIA

c. 1950

LA PAZ GUEST RANCH - PALM SPRINGS, CALIF.

c. 1950

518—A TYPICAL RESIDENTIAL DRIVE IN CALIFORNIA

1A-H377

c. 1945

The Village Street — Palm Canyon Drive, Palm Springs, California

8A-H1286

c. 1950

A Winter Croquet Game at The Desert Inn, Palm Springs, California

9B-H653

c. 1950

Home of George Montgomery and wife Dinah Shore in Palm Springs

K5772

c. 1950

c. 1935

c. 1935

c. 1935

"A wilderness of fateful buffetings . . . swept by seas, shattered by earthquakes and volcanos, beaten by winds and sands, and scorched by suns. Yet . . . out of its desolation it brings forth increase. . . ." (John C. Van Dyke, *The Desert*, 1901)

Bank Bldg.,
El Centro, Cal.

c. 1905

79700 PALM SPRING INDIANS AT HOME, CALIFORNIA.

c. 1925

H-2465 Santa Fe Limited at Needles, California. Indians Selling Beadwork In Front of El Garces Hotel.

c. 1925

2177 Chili (Red Pepper) drying in front of Adobe Home

c. 1940

I wish I were a yucca, a yucca, a yucca
A curly headed yucca, high on a woodsy hill.
I'd drink in desert sunshine,
More sunshine, more sunshine,
Into my creamy blossoms,
As I stood there proud and still.

But I wouldn't be a yucca, a yucca, a yucca
I couldn't be a yucca, unless I knew that you,
And Annabelle and Mother,
And Rose and Baby Brother,
And Tabbycat and Twinkletoes
Could all be yuccas too.

(An entry in a poetry club contest from the Burbank/Glendale
area, circa 1942)

6005   Yucca Whipplei, California.

c. 1915

Missions

SAN GABRIEL BELLS BY NIGHT
FOUNDED 1771

c. 1915

In the eighteenth century, Father Junipero Serra marched up from Mexico, along what is now the California coast. His journeys alone make him remarkable. His route has become the Camino Real, and as he journeyed he paused to set up twenty-one missions between San Diego and Sonoma.

In 1834, French traveler Duflot de Mofras enthused that "more than 30,000 Indian converts were lodged in the Mission buildings, receiving religious culture, assisting at divine worship. . . . Over 400,000 horned cattle pastured upon the plains, as well as 60,000 horses and more than 300,000 sheep, goats and swine. . . . The different Missions rivaled each other in the production of wine, brandy, soap, leather, hides, wool, oil, cotton, hemp, linen, tobacco, salt and soda."

But the mission system carried the seeds of its own destruction. The original buildings had been made of adobe—simply the clay of the neighborhood reinforced with straw—coated on the outside with a thin layer of stucco. They made for handsome edifices and their insulation was perfectly suited to the climate. But they were not earthquake proof.

From the beginning, Spanish explorers were aware of the problem of earthquakes. The Franciscan padres were invariably accompanied by a few Spanish troops, descended from Conquistadors. Each night as they camped, the land would shake beneath them. The terrified military might name their camp "The Place of 2,000 Temblors," but the padres would serenely name the same ground after a saint. . . .

Santa Barbara Mission. California.

c. 1905

1005 – GARDEN OF SANTA BARBARA MISSION, CALIFORNIA.

c. 1915

COPR. DETROIT PUBLISHING CO.

70765 SAN GABRIEL MISSION, CALIFORNIA   FOUNDED 1771

c. 1925

91 – San Gabriel Mission, Founded 1771, California.

c. 1915

c. 1910

c. 1910

Mission Santa Barbara is "the Queen of the Missions." But who has not been captivated by San Juan Capistrano when—on March 19—the swallows come back each year?

c. 1910

San Luis Rey Mission, showing the Court, San Diego County, Cal.

c. 1905

Mission San Miguel, California.

c. 1910

San Diego Mission, California.

c. 1910

1070:—Resting at the Old Well, San Fernando, Mission, Cal.

c. 1930

Oranges And Oil

1883 – A CARLOAD OF MAMMOTH NAVEL ORANGES FROM

S.P. 79265

Copyright 1908 by Edward H. Mitchell, San Francisco.

c. 1909

There seemed no end to Southern California's bounty. To the west, in the Pacific, a metropolis of fish swam around waiting to be caught. To the east, the inhospitable Mojave had enough sand for cement from Colton, Barstow, Victorville, Redlands. Agricultural products poured forth from an almost unimaginable cornucopia of riches. Sugar beets sprouted as far as the eye could see. Almond orchards spread out for acres like mother's best lace tablecloth. Vineyards blanketed the valleys and foothills east of Los Angeles up through Devore and into the Cajon Pass. The desert yielded up an infinity of dates that were sent back east to envious relatives.

But from the turn of the century until World War II, twin symbols of wealth dominated those postal images that Southern California sent eastward–oranges and oil. The pure and simple golden orange bewitched the American imagination–a delicacy so scarce in the rest of the country that a child might count himself lucky if he got one in his Christmas stocking.

Real wealth, oil wealth, lay just under the earth's surface waiting to be discovered by E.L. Doheny in 1892. By the early twenties, this resource had given Southern California a goofy moniker–"Oilderado." Hundreds of investors were willing to put up money in purely speculative ventures with no more than a picture of the land they were investing in. Oil brought a tremendous surge of new capital, most of which eventually paid off in ample returns.

Oil Fields.

c. 1915

California Oil Wells.

c. 1915

1541 – CALIFORNIA OIL WELL ON FIRE.

c. 1915

2251 Reflections in a Lake of Oil.

c. 1915

c. 1935

R-74   THE PARENT NAVEL ORANGE TREE, RIVERSIDE, CALIFORNIA

ORIGINAL TREE BROUGHT FROM BAHIA, BRAZIL, IN 1873   2A-H138

c. 1940

In 1939 alone, California produced thirty-nine million crates of Valencia and Navel oranges. Though oranges are still a part of Southern California's economy, the great sea of groves has given way to homes and industries.

979 — ORANGE PACKING IN CALIFORNIA.

c. 1910

c. 1915

89 - Orange Groves and Snowfields, California.

2987 – An Alfalfa Crop.

The Berry Pickers.

c. 1915

c. 1915

845–DATE PALMS IN CALIFORNIA.

Onion Field in Calif.

c. 1940

c. 1915

349 – A 230 Lb. Pumpkin from California.

c. 1910

Specimen of California Strawberries.

c. 1909

530 – THIS IS HOW WATERMELONS GROW IN CALIFORNIA.

c. 1910

In 1947, Historian Robert Glass Clelend noted that in the previous generation "Americans changed from a...diet of meat, bread, starchy vegetables, and heavy desserts to... fruits, nuts, melons...." California met that need.

Celebrations And Revelries

Tournament of Roses, New Year's Day,
Pasadena, California.
FLORAL FLOAT.

c. 1910

Of course, New York had museums, the opera, the ballet, and nightclubs, but what they sorely lacked back east was Cawston's Ostrich Farm or Gay's Lion Farm or that Alligator Farm where tourists and owners alike seem never to have passed up a chance to take a risky ride.

Southern Californians made their own fun. Pasadena settlers formed the Valley Hunt Club, once bringing a coyote to earth in the post office on Colorado Street. When, later, the Hunt Club destroyed an innocent bystanding cow by mistake, they turned to chariot races. After one too many chariot crashes, Pasadenans turned first to the Rose Parade, then to the football games that went with it. Today, the Rose Parade is seen by millions, but it began modestly enough with homemade floats and bevies of local beauties—a party on the move.

If these amusements seemed small in scope, other celebrants conceived of diversions on a scale far vaster. In 1915 and 1916, the Panama-California Exposition sprang up on the outskirts of the city of San Diego. Twenty years later, the California Pacific International Exposition convened on the same spot. Luxurious and baroque, the buildings commemorating these twin spectacles still stand, reminders of elegance past. North again, outside of Pasadena, Professor Lowe built his famous cog railway. . . . And in 1955, Walt Disney, the greatest entrepreneur and entertainer of them all, inaugurated the apotheosis of all amusement parks, Disneyland itself.

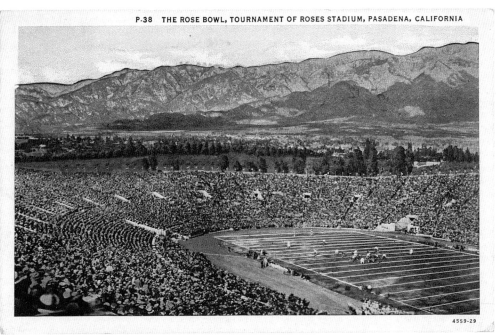

P-38 THE ROSE BOWL, TOURNAMENT OF ROSES STADIUM, PASADENA, CALIFORNIA

4559-29

c. 1925

The Chariot Races, New Years Day, Pasadena, Cal.

c. 1905

California Cutter

c. 1910

In 1896, Pasadena co-opted responsibility for the Tournament of Roses from the Valley Hunt Club, incurring $595 in expenses for all of the "floats." The first Rose Parade was held shortly after the Club's founding in 1888.

Tournament of Roses, New Year's Day, Pasadena, California.

c. 1915

Pasadena's Tournament of Roses on New Year's Day.

c. 1915

Floral Parade, Tournament of Roses, New Year's Day, Pasadena, Cal.

c. 1915

Floral Entry, Pasadena Tournament of Roses

c. 1920

c. 1910

Tournament of Roses,
New Year's Day,
Pasadena, California.
FLORAL FLOAT.

PANAMA-CALIFORNIA EXPOSITION 1915
San Diego California
View from Balboa Park

c. 1915

5401. Prado from West Gate,
Panama-California International Exposition,
San Diego, Cal.

c. 1915

PANAMA-CALIFORNIA EXPOSITION, SAN DIEGO, CALIFORNIA, 1915.

71657 PIGEONS ON THE PLAZA DE PANAMA, IN FRONT OF SACRAMENTO VALLEY BUILDING

c. 1915

PANAMA-CALIFORNIA EXPOSITION, SAN DIEGO, CAL. 1915.

LAGOONS IN FRONT OF BOTANICAL BUILDING.

c. 1915

c. 1930

Fontana's
Prize Winning Exhibit
National Orange Show, San Bernardino, 1913

c. 1930

758 - One of California's Golden Products.

c. 1911

In 1911, a group of citrus-growers gathered beneath a tent and invented the San Bernardino Orange Show. Three hundred came that first year. Now the ten-day extravaganza draws over a quarter of a million annually.

c. 1930

"The lion is vulgarly known as the King of Beasts," Charles Gay was fond of remarking. "He is far from it. Many animals surpass him in intelligence. He is practically untameable, and always treacherous. But he is courageous and majestic."

c. 1915

c. 1915

c. 1915

PRIZE WINNERS, CAWSTON OSTRICH FARM, SOUTH PASADENA, CALIF.

Snowballing and Sledding in Winter, Mt. Lowe, Cal.

c. 1915

Circular Bridge, Mt. Lowe, California. Elevation, 4200 Feet

c. 1915

The Mt. Lowe cog railway, "The Greatest Mountain Trolley Trip in the World," was built by Professor Thaddeus Sobieski Caulincourt Lowe—an early balloonist—and rose 3,130 feet in 5.54 miles. It opened in 1893, eventually including an observatory, a zoo, four hotels, a miniature golf course, tennis, shuffleboard and the world's largest search light.

c. 1915

c. 1955

Paradise

The Palisades, Santa Monica, California.

c. 1910

By gad! It's Paradise!" Lucky Baldwin said, when he first saw the San Gabriel Valley. Faced with the task of defining Southern California to the folks back home, the western traveler resorted to images of the idyllic, the lyrical, the supranatural. A railroad car flanked by orange trees. A map of the United States in which the sun shone only on California. The world's biggest rose bush. A panorama sweeping from sunlit surf to sun-capped mountains. Everything here bespoke innocently provocative pleasure. Lissome beauties, who seemed to combine virtue and sensuality, peeked out of rose arbors, frolicked in the waves, and posed among those oranges so much like the sun.

This was paradise but not simply for the rich. If movie stars had set up in palaces, why, then, the common man could make a palace of his own. An adobe fortress that saluted the Franciscan fathers. A hillside residence (from which you could see Catalina). A modest Cape Cod cottage literally drenched in roses. When Andrew Marvell wrote his metaphysical poem, "Little T.C. in a Prospect of Flowers," he could never have dreamed of the almost demented display of nature that a person might buy—"Hydranges in front of a Cal. Residence"—and send home to disbelievers who still lived in a rain-soaked, dreary world. No wonder Southern Californians were accused of bragging—they might have been. But seen in a kinder light, these excesses reflected a sincere desire to describe what was—to them—a heaven on earth.

4600. Torrey Pines and Del Mar in the Distance, San Diego, Cal.

c. 1910

Sure is the life for me, nothing to do, but eat, and am doing that. Sun is out bright this morning, so we will be on a go, some where. Suppose you have sampled the dates by now. Earnest

Mr & Mrs Gilbert Taplin
Miles
Iowa

POST CARD

c. 1945

An Artistic Moorish Type California Residence.

c. 1910

For years, newcomers made it a habit to laugh at the extravagance of California architecture, but the impulse to build these edifices came from the most exalted aspect of the human condition—the determined belief that one's most cherished dreams could become manifest.

California Poppies

These Golden Poppies I send you
From California---where they grew.

Copyright 1908 by M. Rieder.

c. 1908

A California Residence.

c. 1910

LA-128. A TROPICAL PARK IN SOUTHERN CALIFORNIA.

101704

c. 1920

c. 1910

Hydranges in front of a Cal. Residence.

c. 1915

76 Washed Ashore, as the Camera Clicked, Venice, Cal.

c. 1918

c. 1915

"There is a climate here to suit everyone.... It is not an enervating climate, but bracing and full of electricity; a climate that makes the sick well and the strong more vigorous." (A Los Angeles Chamber of Commerce brochure, 1921.)

Acknowledgements

Tourists Departing from Tia Juana, Mexico, for San Diego, Cal.

c. 1905

INTERNATIONAL BOUNDARY LINE BETWEEN U. S. AND MEXICO, 16 MILES SOUTH OF SAN DIEGO, CALIFORNIA—85

c. 1950

Monica Highland wishes to ac knowledge her debt to the factual information taken from either th published work or conversations of Jacques Barzun, Robert Glas Cleland, Bruce Henstell, Christopher Isherwood, Gernot Kuehn Maureen Michelson & Michael Dressler, Robert Miles Parker, Na Sherman, Jack Smith, Benjamin F. Stelter, John C. Van Dyke, Evely Waugh, Matt Weinstock, Glenn Larson & Bruce Belland, John Weave and Fodor/California; and the fiction of Paul Cain, Raymond Chandle and John Steinbeck. She has drawn on her extended family's suppor including memories of the late George Laws and F. See On, as well a the living assistance of Richard Kendall, Lynda Laws, Bob Laws an Clara Sturak. She could scarcely exist without the presence of Caroly See, Lisa See Kendall, and John Espey.

Beyond all these, she gives special thanks to Jack Miles who started all, to Ann Caiger from the Department of Special Collections of th UCLA Research Library for her patience; to the splendid projec director of this volume, Alison Morba, for her enthusiastic encourage ment; and to Jean Andrews for her editing which was as patient as it wa meticulous. And, of course, Monica would have had no postcards o which to base this book without the golden age of the postcard industr with its photographers, hand tinters, printers, and collectors.